D0909313

Women Shaping History

Cover by Jackie Denison

Library of Congress Number: 79-13734

1 2 3 4 5 6 7 8 9 0 83 82 81 80 79

Printed and bound in the United States of America.

Library of Congress Cataloging in Publication Data
DeClue, Denise.
   Women shaping history.
   Bibliography: p. 48.
   SUMMARY: Presents brief biographies of women
prominent in women's movements, including Lucretia
Mott, Lucy Stone, Elizabeth Cady Stanton, and Gloria
Steinem
   1. Feminists—United States—Biography—Juvenile
literature. [1. Feminists] I. Title.
HQ1412.D4   301.41'2'0922 [B] [920]   79-13734
ISBN 0-8172-1380-5

WOMEN
SHAPING HISTORY

Denise DeClue

RAINTREE PUBLISHERS
Milwaukee • Toronto • Melbourne • London

CONTENTS

4

INTRODUCTION

A little more than ten years ago, hardly anyone had heard of "women's lib." There was no "liberation movement" for women. But there were always women who wanted more out of life. Some women found that caring for a husband, a home and a family was not enough to make them happy. For the most part, these women struggled alone.

There were times in history when women signed men's names to their paintings. Women authors used men's names for their work in order to sell what they had written. Some women were able to have both a family and a career, but they were often told that they were "cheating" their husbands and children by doing this. Some women never married and were called "pushy career girls" or "old maids." Often, these women felt that there was something wrong with them. Other women, who settled down to become housewives and mothers, often felt there was something wrong with them, too. They didn't feel fulfilled doing what society said they were *supposed* to do. They felt used. **2092704**

During several periods in United States history, women joined together and took a hard look at the way things were: first, in the 1800s, when they were fighting for the right to vote, and more recently in the 1960s and 1970s — with the growth of the modern women's liberation movement for equal rights. These women discovered that there wasn't anything wrong with them; they decided that society was wrong. Women simply weren't being treated like full human beings.

For years they didn't have the right to vote or to own property. The law regarded married women as property of their husbands. In 1920, women won the right to vote. But they were still treated differently than men: by their ministers, their teachers, their governments and their families. Women were protected. Many were treated like fragile dolls. They were taught to be quiet and humble and to make life easier for men, who were doing the really "important" things. Most women were told that being a mother was the most important thing they could be. But they found themselves telling people that they were "just housewives." They were taught, from an early age, that this was a "man's world" — and their place in it was at home.

Women were taught that they should be "feminine" — which means "womanly" according to the dictionary. Most women knew that "feminine" didn't really mean "weak." But the books and magazines, and sometimes their mothers, told them this was the way to get a man. This was the way to be happy.

The women's movement helped to change the way women felt about themselves and the way men felt about women. Some women began to call themselves "feminists," women who demand the same rights as men. Women began to see that they had something in common with all other women: rich, poor, black, Chicano, and white. They agreed to work together so that all people could be equal.

This is the story of women who worked together to change things. It is the story of women who fought for the freedom to be themselves and for the freedom for *you* to *choose* the kind of life you'd like to lead and the kind of work you'd like to do.

The Bettmann Archive

COLONIAL WOMEN AND EARLY FEMINISTS

I do not believe that there was any community in which the souls of some women were not beating their wings in rebellion. For my . . . self I can say that every fibre of my being rebelled, although silently, all the hours that I sat and sewed gloves for a miserable pittance which, as it was earned, could never by mine. I wanted to work, but I wanted to choose my task and I wanted to collect my wages.

Charlotte Woodward

America, that land across the ocean, was rich. The forests were full of game, and the lakes and rivers were brimming with fish. There was gold in the hills, and there was land and opportunity — enough for everyone who came.

The men — explorers, trappers, fishermen — came long before the women. But London merchants wanted to build a stable, money-making colony in Virginia; they wanted the men to settle down and stay in one place. So, in 1619, they sent over a boatload of ninety women, guaranteed them husbands, and hoped that the "gentler sex" would tame the wild adventurers. A year later, eighteen women and eleven girls arrived on the Pilgrim's boat, the Mayflower.

Life was not easy in the colonies. Men and women worked together clearing forests and building homes. Yet there were important differences in the rights men and women had. A married woman gave up her civil rights, or personal liberties, to her husband. She could not sign contracts or own property, and she had no right to her own earnings. She could not vote, and divorce was almost unheard of. The church, the government, and the men treated married women like slaves or children.

Unmarried women probably suffered more. They could earn only a fraction of what men could earn, and they were discouraged from taking jobs outside the home. There were a few schools for women, but the subjects taught were mainly womanly arts such as sewing and weaving.

For the millions of black women who were snatched from their African homes, forced into stinking slave ships, and sold on southern slave auction blocks, there was often not even the opportunity to choose a mate.

Anne Hutchinson, who moved to Boston with her family around 1634, was one of the first colonial women to speak out for what she believed in. She was a religious woman of the Calvinist faith. But she had come to believe a little differently than the men who ran her church. They believed that only ministers could have special relationships with God. And only men, of course, could be ministers. But Anne Hutchinson believed that God dwelled in every human being, that each person, man or woman, had a special relationship with Him. Groups of women, and sometimes men, began meeting at Mistress Hutchinson's house to hear her speak about "the indwelling Christ."

The heads of the church were furious. They brought Anne Hutchinson to trial for heresy — for taking a different point of view about their religion. They attacked Anne Hutchinson in civil court and in religious proceedings. Even though she was pregnant at the time of her civil trial, and seriously ill, they made her stand rather than sit, until she nearly collapsed. She was found guilty and was banished from the colony. She fled with her family to Pelham Bay on the outskirts of New York City.

Anne Hutchinson stood up for what she believed in, at a time when women were not suposed to speak out at all. With only her knowledge of the Bible and her belief in her own convictions, she challenged the best-educated minds in her colony. She did not win the rights she sought, but she did win the respect of many, and a place in our history books.

WOMEN WORKING TOGETHER

The earliest women's organizations didn't have much to do with "women's liberation," but from the beginning of America's history, women joined together to get things done. During the Revolutionary War, the Daughters of Liberty helped the cause by refusing to buy English goods. They worked together to spin and weave so they would not be dependent on the British for cloth. Betsy Ross is famous for making the first American flag, but she was only one of hundreds of revolutionary women who used their sewing talents to help the war effort. Many women met at the home of Benjamin Franklin's daughter, Sara Bache, to cut and sew shirts for the army. One visitor reported seeing some 2,200 newly-made and freshly-starched shirts ready for shipment to the troops.

After the war, women worked together in church sewing circles to raise money for missionary or charitable work. In the 1820s, there were groups like the Female Improvement Society, which met each week to read what they called "useful books" and to share their personal writings. There were also groups of black women like the Ohio Ladies Education society, which worked to establish schools for black children. But female antislavery societies were the most active women's groups in nineteenth-century America.

The question of slavery had been heating up for a century. Slave trade had been banned in 1808, but illegal ships still arrived with human cargo, and slaves were still sold. And while the South insisted its economy depended on slave labor, Northerners were increasingly outraged. Groups of people who called themselves abolitionists were determined to end the practice of slavery in this country.

In 1833, the American Anti-Slavery Society, an all-male group, met in Philadelphia. They permitted a few women to attend. But the women could not speak at the meetings or join the society. After the convention, twenty women met to form the Philadelphia Female Anti-Slavery Society. Similar groups started up in other states, and in 1837, the first female National Anti-Slavery Society met in New York with eighty-one delegates from twelve states. These women were courageous. There were strong pro-slavery feelings in the North, as well as in the South; and the very notion of women meeting together and making speeches and planning actions, made many men angry. Mobs of violent men sometimes broke up their meetings.

Sarah and Angelina Grimke were two sisters who pioneered the way for women in public life. They grew up on a plantation in South Carolina, where their family had owned slaves. The Grimke sisters had always hated slavery, and when they moved north in 1836, they became friends with many people who were abolitionists. They were asked to speak at an anti-slavery meeting, and the stories they told of the horrors of slavery moved many people to tears.

They were asked to speak at other meetings, but there was one big problem — women weren't supposed to speak before a public audience. The common belief at the time was that a woman's place was in the home, with her children. Church

Sarah Grimke   Angelina Grimke

groups and politicians complained that the Grimke sisters were unwomanly, un-Christian, and immodest.

The sisters fought back. They began to speak about the equality of women. Some of the abolitionist men feared their speeches would hurt the anti-slavery movement by angering those people who didn't believe that women should speak in public. But Angelina stood firm. How could women help end slavery, she asked, if they were forced into silence by men?

All over New England, women tramped miles through the snow to hear the sisters speak. "We abolitionist women," said Angelina, "are turning this world upside down."

In the summer of 1840, American abolitionists traveled to London, England, for the world Anti-

Slavery Society convention. But after a hot debate, the men decided not to admit women delegates. The women had to sit quietly in the galleries and watch. Two of those American women, Lucretia Mott and Elizabeth Cady Stanton, met outside after the meeting and talked. How could men talk about equal rights for slaves when they wouldn't even let women talk at their meetings?

Lucretia Mott was the young wife of an abolitionist leader. She grew up on an island off Cape Cod, Massachusetts, where most of the men worked on whaling boats. A strong tradition of women's equality existed there because the women had to take care of business while their husbands were at sea. Lucretia's father ran a whaling ship; her mother ran a store.

Lucretia's family belonged to the Quaker faith, one of the few religions which allowed women to speak in public. She taught at a Quaker school for a while and when she was twenty-eight, she was ordained a Quaker minister. Thus she was one of the first women to gain experience in public speaking.

Elizabeth Cady Stanton was the daughter of a judge. As a child, she spent many hours in her father's office, sitting quietly and listening to the people who came to talk to him about their legal problems. She remembered how her father sometimes gave his own money to help women whose husbands had hurt them. For example, a woman's husband might sell property she had inherited, or he might steal wages she had earned — if she

14

Elizabeth Cady Stanton Lucretia Mott

worked. There was nothing these women could legally do to protect their rights, and Elizabeth Cady Stanton would not forget.

When she met Lucretia Mott in London, they decided there should be a meeting on women's rights. Women should work together to declare their independence from men and to gain legal equality. But it would be eight long years before the women could arrange such a convention.

Elizabeth returned to America and moved to Seneca Falls, New York, with her husband. She stayed home, washed and ironed, cooked and cleaned, and took care of her brood of children. She was a brilliant woman, and she became discouraged with the drudgery and loneliness of housework. She was convinced that women should have more opportunities and be able to make the same choices as men.

When Lucretia Mott came to visit her in 1848, the women decided to hold the meeting they had talked about eight years before.

Some three hundred people, including forty men, went to the meeting. They rode in horse-drawn wagons as many as fifty miles to attend. They wrote and signed a "Declaration of Sentiments" based on the Declaration of Independence. In their declaration, they demanded that women have the right to equal education, to speak and write publicly, and to be equal with men in business. And, they demanded the right to vote.

This first American Women's Rights Convention marked the beginning of the women's movement. It would be a long time before women actually won the vote, but at that 1848 meeting in Seneca Falls, they agreed to fight.

WINNING THE VOTE

After the Civil War broke out in 1865, feminists, like other women, were busy taking care of the wounded and keeping their homes together while the men were away at war. But after the fighting was over, and the country was mending, they began to speak out again.

Getting the vote was not going to be easy. Since they couldn't vote, elections wouldn't do them any good. The women wanted amendments to the state constitutions and to the U.S. Constitution, but they had to get the Congress*men*, who were elected by other *men*, to make the changes. Thousands of women and some men signed petitions — papers stating that women should be able to vote — which were sent to the legislators. The women were called suffragettes because they wanted "suffrage" which means the right to vote.

Lucy Stone was one of the most popular suffragettes. She traveled around the country, making speeches and passing out petitions. Sometimes people expected to see a rough, manly woman, smoking a cigar and stomping around in boots. They thought that if women wanted the same rights as men, they probably wanted to be like men. Imagine their surprise when a small and dainty Lucy Stone, wearing a black satin dress with a lacy collar, rose to speak. She was not "unwomanly" at all.

But eventually Lucy Stone did something shocking. She rebelled against the clothing fashions of the day. She said that women could hardly breathe in the tightly-laced corsets they usually wore, that their heavy skirts and petticoats made it hard to walk and picked up all kinds of garbage from the streets. She and Elizabeth Stanton started wearing a new kind of outfit — the bloomer dress.

Lucy Stone

Women never wore pants in those days, even at home, so this loose and funny-looking outfit offended many men. Rather than distract attention from the real cause — suffrage — they finally gave up the freedom and comfort of the bloomers and went back to wearing their other clothes.

The fight for the vote continued. Susan B. Anthony and other New York women collected 6,000 signatures in ten weeks. Carrie Chapman Catt, an Iowa newspaper woman, and other women worked hard in all parts of the country.

Men laughed at them, asking how could women, who liked to be carried over mud puddles and lifted into carriages, be trusted with the vote. Even some women, who were afraid that they would lose the comforts of home if they got the vote, were against it. A lot of people still believed that women weren't as smart or as strong as men, that they needed to be taken care of, like children.

A proud black feminist named Sojourner Truth told them they had it all wrong about women: "Look at my arm! I have plowed and planted and gathered into barns . . . and ain't I a woman? I

Sojourner Truth

could work as much and eat as much as a man —
when I could get it — and bear the lash as well!
And ain't I a woman? I have borne thirteen children
and seen most of 'em sold into slavery, and when I
cried out with my mother's grief, none but Jesus
heard me — and ain't I a woman?"

In 1914, World War I broke out in Europe, and
when it was over, the women were still campaign-
ing for the vote. Finally, in 1920, after hundreds
and hundreds of state and national campaigns,
after thousands of parades and meetings and
speeches and petitions, thirty-six states ratified the
Nineteenth Amendment to the United States Constitution, and women won the right to vote.

These suffragettes from the Salvation Army marched to Washington, D.C., to help win the vote for women. The group was led by Rosalie Jones (center).

20

FLAPPERS, HOUSEWIVES, AND MODERN FEMINISTS

It was a strange stirring, a sense of dissatisfaction . . . each suburban wife struggled with it alone. As she made the beds, shopped for groceries, matched slipcover material, ate peanut butter sandwiches with her children, chauffeured Cub Scouts and Brownies . . . she was afraid to ask even of herself the silent question — "Is this all?"

Betty Friedan

After they won the vote, women were full citizens of the United States, but in many ways they were "second-class" citizens. They still didn't have the same rights as men. You would think that after winning the vote, women would have fought for other rights. They still weren't guaranteed equal pay for equal work. They still couldn't get the jobs they wanted. Many of the best colleges still didn't allow women students.

But the feminists were tired of fighting. Many

21

women felt that they could now vote to change the laws and that they should pay attention to other causes. So they worked for human rights. They worked with unions in the labor movement — for workers who were badly treated by their bosses. They worked for new laws that would protect children who were treated badly in factories. They worked for freedom for black people, who had been freed from slavery after the Civil War, but who were still not free to live and work as they wanted.

In the 1920s, some women, especially the college girls, decided to free themselves from old styles and customs. They threw out their long skirts, and "bobbed" (cut) their long hair. They went out at night in the new "horseless carriages" — automobiles. They went out alone with boys, without chaperones — a habit that made their grandmothers shudder. They drank beer with their boyfriends and took jobs outside the home. Some people called them "flappers" because of the floppy galoshes (boots) they wore unbuckled and flapping. Others called them "hussies" and bad girls. The flappers were trying out personal freedoms long denied their mothers and older sisters. They wanted to experience as much of life as they could. "Why should women sit home and wait for someone to ask them to marry?" they asked. "Why shouldn't we have some fun?"

For many, the fun didn't last very long. There still weren't many good jobs for women. And, even though more women received advanced edu-

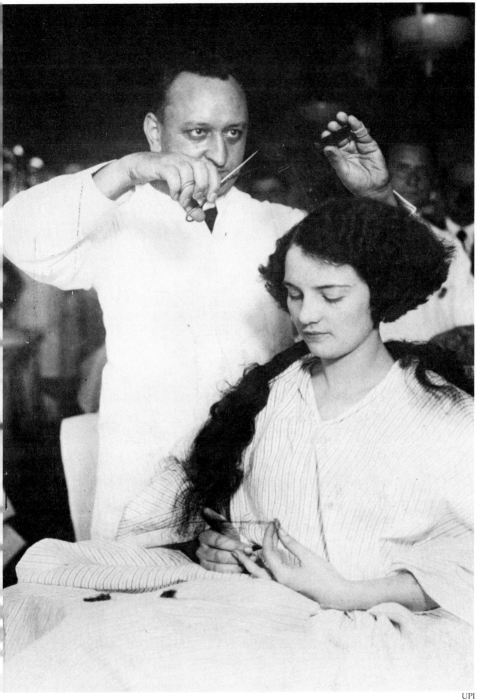

During the 1920's, women rebelled against old styles
that had been followed for many years. The woman above
is having her hair cut, or bobbed.

cational degrees in 1930 than ever before, many found themselves working as low-paid secretaries and clerks. In 1929, the stock market crashed and hard times set in. Businesses went broke. During the depression years, thousands and thousands of people lost their jobs. Often women were the first to be fired. There was a feeling that men worked to support their families and women worked "for fun." So, often when women were hired, their wages were less than men's for the same kind of work.

Then, in the 1940s, the United States went to war. Nearly sixteen million men left their jobs and their families to fight in Europe against Adolph Hitler and in the Pacific against the Japanese. While the men were gone, many women were needed to work in factories, making guns and air-planes to fight the war. More than six million women worked during the war years. They packed their lunches, put on overalls, and took their chil-dren to the more than 3,100 day care centers the government set up. Because they were really needed, the newspapers didn't make as much fun of working women as they had in the past.

When the men came home after the war, people were ready to settle down, have families, and make their lives normal again. Many of the women left their jobs forever. Others joked that they were going to college to get an "M.R.S. degree" — a husband to take care of them. And slowly, the old ideas that women weren't as good as men — that their *only* place was in the home — grew back in people's minds.

EQUAL RIGHTS FOR ALL PEOPLE

There were always some women who wanted more opportunities and choices out of life, for themselves and for all people. During the late 1950s and early 1960s, these women joined with other women to form a "movement" — a group of people all working for the same idea of change.

Group efforts for equal rights began with the civil rights movement in the late 1950s. Some city governments had set up two kinds of schools — one for blacks and one for whites. This segregation was based on a "separate but equal ruling" made by local courts. The United States Supreme Court, however, said that "separate" was not "equal" — that everyone, black and white, male and female, had a right to go to the public school of his or her choice.

Many people saw the obvious problems that black people had, such as low-paying jobs, poor educations, and housing laws that kept them from moving into neighborhoods they liked. Many men and women supported the civil rights movement — working for personal liberties for all people — and it helped improve conditions for black people.

One of the problems in the late 1950s and early 1960s was that some white people believed that black people should be "kept in their places" — meaning that they were not as good as white people. Women in the civil rights movement began to realize that many men had similar attitudes about women. And, that women, in fact, had certain attitudes about themselves that served to keep them "in their place."

Women in the 1960s learned from the civil rights movement, just as their sisters in the 1840s and 1850s learned from the abolitionist movement. They learned that they could work together to change things. They learned that they didn't have to accept the place society put them in — that society wasn't always right. They learned that they were not the only ones unhappy with the way things were.

THE FEMININE MYSTIQUE

Something happened to American women in the 1930s, 1940s, and 1950s. Author Betty Friedan wrote about this "something" in a book called *The Feminine Mystique*, which was published in 1963.

Betty Friedan wrote that for many years the doctors and psychiatrists, and teachers and women's magazine writers had been telling women that their goal in life was to be truly feminine. And, being feminine meant knowing how to get a man and keep him, how to take care of babies, how to buy a dishwasher, bake bread, and how to look and act like a lady.

Women, she wrote, were in a no-win situation. Of course they wanted to be womanly and attractive, and they wanted to be liked and loved. Of course many wanted to marry and have children. But was that enough? Betty Friedan traveled the country and talked to hundreds of women — married women with children, who were doing everything "right." They were doing wonderful "jobs" as mothers and wives. But something was

© Bettye Lane

Betty Friedan is shown giving a speech during a march on 5th Avenue in New York City in 1970.

wrong. They were not happy.

"My days are busy, and dull, too," said one young wife. "All I ever do is mess around. I get up at eight — I make breakfast, so I do the dishes, have lunch, do some more dishes, and some laundry and cleaning in the afternoon. Then it's supper dishes and I get to sit down a few minutes, before the children have to be sent to bed . . . That's all there is to my day. It's just like any other wife's day. Humdrum. The biggest time, I am chasing kids."

Millions of women read Betty Friedan's book in the 1960s and early 1970s and many of them cried with relief. At last the problem they secretly felt was brought out in the open. At last they knew that other women felt the same way they did. They realized that the "feminine mystique" had taught them that they should be happy being housewives. They realized that they were not the only ones who wanted more out of life.

Betty Friedan's book helped to change many women's lives. Some found that by going back to work they could fulfill themselves. Others found that their children were happier when they were happier, even if they weren't around all the time. Some decided that there was nothing wrong with not wanting to get married. Many began to learn about their cars, plumbing, and politics. They decided that they didn't want to be dependent on men anymore.

CONSCIOUSNESS RAISING

Women began to take a long, hard look at the "double standard" — a set of standards which apply differently to one group of people than to another — which society applied to men and women. Men, they thought, can be married, have children, and work at jobs they like, too. Why can't women? An unmarried man is a bachelor, they reasoned, but why call an unmarried woman an "old maid"?

Women met together in "consciousness raising"

groups where they studied the history of women and the history of the women's rights movement. They thought about their roles in society and the way they had been taught that women should behave.

"I work," one might say, "and when I get home my husband expects me to put his supper on the table. I'm as tired as he is. I think he should cook once in awhile."

"I'm better at my boss's job than my boss is," another might add. "But he makes me bring him coffee. I feel like a waitress or a slave. I'm afraid if I say something, he'll fire me."

Still another woman might add: "I have never worked outside the home at all. I got married before I finished college and I was busy with babies for years. But now all my children are in school, and all I do is wait on them. I want something else from life, but I don't know where to start."

These women — high school girls, young wives, older married women, unmarried women — gave each other support. They began to feel like sisters. They began to plan "actions" — ways to get men and other women to start seeing the way things really were. They had parades and rallies. They walked into "all-male" bars and clubs. They printed posters and hung them wherever they could.

A lot of people wanted women to stay home and cook and clean and take care of their children. They liked things just the way they were — especially the men. But the women in what had come to be known as the women's liberation movement were convinced that the world would be a better place if all people — men, women, blacks, whites, Latinos, the rich and the poor — had equal rights and equal opportunities.

THE NATIONAL ORGANIZATION FOR WOMEN

Many of the women's actions centered on changing the way people thought, but they also worked to change the laws. Betty Friedan went to Washington, D.C. to lobby for an amendment to the Civil Rights Act of 1964. Women wanted an amendment that said women, as well as blacks, must be treated equally under the law. The amendment passed and the government set up the Equal Employment Opportunity Commission (EEOC) to enforce the law.

But the EEOC didn't do very much for women's rights. The agency didn't pay enough attention to women's complaints about discrimination in hiring practices or on the job. Betty Friedan and other women decided that they needed a national organization of women to push the EEOC to enforce the law. They started The National Organization for Women (NOW).

NOW started out with some dramatic actions. Women walked into the New York EEOC office with signs saying "EEOC has no guts." They staged a sit-in at a popular hotel with a dining room that only served men. The women walked in, sat down, and refused to leave. Newspapers printed stories about these women and people began to think about the unfairness of clubs and dining rooms that wouldn't serve women. Why not? Weren't women just as good as men?

NOW also began to study the other problems faced by women in the 1960s. NOW members studied education, jobs, health, and the media (newspapers, magazines, books, television and movies). Their studies resulted in facts and figures showing just how unfair things were for women.

Jobs. NOW found that women, on the average, only earned sixty percent (a little over half) of what men earned. There were many more women in low-paying jobs than men.

And, women in professional jobs seldom advanced as quickly, or as often, as men. Even teachers, who were mostly women, were stuck at the lower-paying jobs, while men "moved up the ladder" to the better jobs. Nine out of every ten grade school teachers were women. Only twenty percent of the college teachers were women.

Businessmen and employers gave all sorts of reasons why women had the worst jobs. Women weren't qualified, they said. Women didn't have enough experience or education. Besides, they said, the women would just quit to get married and have babies anyway, so why hire them in the first place? But the problem that wasn't discussed was that many men believed that women couldn't do their jobs as well as men. And also many bosses didn't think men would like the idea of working for a woman.

Education. The NOW education study group found that two-thirds of all the college drop-outs were women. Hardly any of the history books had information about great women. Even beginning reading books mostly showed "Daddies" as the strong, smart, active people, and "Mommies" as weaker, dumber, quieter people. From an early age little girls were learning not to compete, to be passive and quiet.

The Media. NOW studied the image of women presented on television, in books, movies, magazines and newspapers. They discovered that women were mostly shown at home. Hardly any women doctors, lawyers, or judges were shown on television. Most movies dealt with women as "sex objects" — pretty things to be shown off or used by men. Newspapers used phrases like "shapely blond" when describing women, but they never called a man a "well-built redhead."

The Law. NOW found that there were still many laws on the books from the time when wives were considered the property of their husbands. Some of these laws set out to protect women, but often they cut back women's rights. State laws often discriminated against women. For example, there were rules requiring women to have their husband's approval before they could borrow money or buy property.

Actions. In 1967, the women of NOW met for a convention in Washington, D.C. They passed a

"Bill of Rights" for women. Some of the rights they demanded include: (1) passage of the Equal Rights Constitutional Amendment, which reads in part, "Equality of rights under the law shall not be denied or abridged by the United States or by any State on account of sex"; (2) that men and women, and all races, be given equal chances for jobs and that they get equal pay for equal work; (3) that education be equal and "unsegregated" — separation by sex or race in schools would not be allowed.

In 1970, a group of about one hundred women walked into the offices of the *Ladies Home Journal* magazine and staged a sit-in. They complained that men chose the stories printed in the magazine, and that the stories did not deal with some of the real problems women were facing. Although one out of every three adult women in America was single, divorced, or widowed, the magazine mainly ran stories about women who were wives and mothers. After the women had spent eleven hours in the offices of the publisher, the magazine agreed to print a supplement called "The New Feminism." The supplement made an impact on thousands of women who had never heard of the ideas of the women's liberation movement. It had articles about working women, problems with child care, and a Housewife's Bill of Rights. There were stories about men and women doing housework together and about marriages in which no one was "the boss."

On August 26, 1970, the Women's Liberation Movement and NOW called a National Strike Day. It had been fifty years since women had won the vote, and women took the day off work to

Gloria Steinem, a leader of the women's movement, is answering questions at a news conference. Behind her is a cover of *Ms. Magazine*, of which she is an editor.

celebrate in parades and rallies and demonstrations. Women were findig strength in the movement — the strength to stand up to their bosses and the strength to change their lives. After the strike day, a survey showed that four out of every five people over the age of eighteen had read or heard about the women's liberation movement.

Ms. Magazine. In 1971, there were a number of feminist newspapers. But there wasn't a big, national magazine that spoke about the problems of modern, liberated women. Some of the magazines, like *Ladies Home Journal*, had changed a bit as a result of the movement. But women like journalist Gloria Steinem felt there was a real need for a new magazine. She, and other women, met many times in 1971 and planned for a new magazine. In 1972, the first issue appeared. The 300,000 magazines printed were supposed to be on sale for eight weeks. But they sold out in eight days. And, 20,000 women from all over the country wrote letters of praise to the new magazine. It was one of the biggest responses any magazine had ever received. *Ms. Magazine* was off to a successful beginning.

Why is it called *Ms. Magazine?* And why do feminists use that form of address before their names? For nearly twenty years some secretaries have been using the term "Ms." when addressing letters to women, who might or might not be married. Instead of guessing "Miss" or "Mrs." they'd just put "Dear Ms. Jones."

Feminists thought this was a good idea, since the male form of address, "Mr.", can mean either a married or an unmarried man. The women starting the new magazine thought it fair to provide this kind of equal treatment for women. The term "Ms." means a female human being, they said. It could mean a married woman or an unmarried woman.

SEX ROLES

Once upon a time, long, long ago and far, far away . . . a woman lived with her two daughters and her step-daughter. The woman loved her older daughters and treated them well, but she made her step-daughter, Cinderella, do all the work.

Poor Cinderella! She seemed doomed to an unhappy life. Then her fairy godmother appeared and magically changed her into a beautiful princess with a fancy hairdo, rich clothes, and glass slippers. She went to the ball in style and danced with the handsome prince. He loved her at first sight, and when she ran away, he looked for her all over his kingdom. When he found her, he took her away, married her, and "they lived happily ever after."

Or did they? During the 1960s and 1970s, feminists looked hard at old stories and fairy tales like Cinderella. Just what is the Cinderella story saying? they asked. It doesn't show most girls and women as very nice people. First, the wicked stepmother and the two older sisters are mean, cruel, greedy, and vain. The older sisters are ugly, or at least not pretty. And they act uglier. Then there's Cinderella. What a poor, weak, passive creature she is! You don't see her going off to night school to study so she can get a job to support herself and leave home. You don't see her standing up for her rights at all. She needs magic to change her life. And what kind of magic does she get? Fancy clothes, makeup, and an expensive coach. Is the story telling us that we need these kind of things to "get a man"? Is the story telling us only a "handsome prince" can make us happy? Is the story telling us to be meek and passive and wait for magic to change our lives?

It's fun to read fairy tales, but good luck to the girl who believes in them. The world usually doesn't

In 1977, feminists in Italy demonstrated against a group of youths who had kidnapped a woman. They are forming the symbol of "woman" with their hands.

work that way. Feminists started looking at a lot of books and stories that grade school girls were reading. Again and again, they found the same old stories. Boys were shown to be curious, adventuresome, and clever. Girls were shown in pretty dresses, playing quiet games, and waiting for handsome princes. There were lots of stories about boys growing up to be firemen, engineers, scientists, carpenters, and farmers. And there were lots of stories about girls — growing up to be mommies.

These constant differences between activities for boys and girls were called sex role stereotyping by women in the liberation movement. Stereotyping is an overly simple way of looking at things, which strips humans of individuality. The stories in which the men were always active and the women were always passive — showing the men at work and the women at home — had stereotyped the roles of men and women. Some women may stay at home to raise children, but not all women do. And, besides, some men may want to stay at home and take care of the children.

People who think in stereotypes don't give other human beings a full chance to be themselves. And girls and women who think of themselves as stereotypes don't give themselves a chance to grow. Feminists say that sexual stereotypes trap people into roles in which they're unhappy and uncomfortable. Feminists believe that boys and girls are alike in many ways. For example, they may both like sports and adventure. They may like to run in the wind. They may like to dress up in silly costumes. sometimes boys are unhappy, and sometimes they cry. Sometimes girls get angry and hit somebody. The stereotypes just don't give a true picture of the way things are.

Over the past few years a lot of work has been done to improve schoolbooks. Many of the newer books show girls and boys with the same dreams and ambitions. There are women's history courses at some high schools and many colleges.

Gradually the image of women presented by the media is changing too. There are still, however, a lot of television shows and commercials that stereotype women as dizzy, beautiful dumbbells, cranky old maids, or shrill, mean career girls. But now they are also policewomen, women detectives, businesswomen and unmarried career women.

Improvements in other areas have happened too. More and more women are entering professions which, in the past, were considered male professions. There are more women in law school and medical school than ever before. More than half of the women in the country who have children also work at jobs outside the home. Gradually they are asking, then demanding, that their husbands take some of the responsibility for housework.

Women are more involved in politics, too. Considering that women make up fifty-one percent of the population, however, the number of elected women officials is still small. But women like Shirley Chisolm, a U.S. representative from New York who ran for president in 1970, have made a big impact on the country.

CHANGING TIMES

The issues aren't going to go away, and neither are we. There is change everywhere. We are just beginning.

Bella Abzug

More than fifteen years have passed since the modern women's movement first began. Now almost everybody has heard of "women's lib." And there are a lot of women whose lives have changed because of it. Many women believe they have more choices than ever before. But they also feel that there is still a lot to be done. The Equal Rights Amendment to the United States Constitution was passed by Congress in March, 1972. Thirty-eight states must ratify, or approve, the amendment before it becomes law.

Supporters of the Equal Rights Amendment (ERA) believe it will protect women against laws and practices which treat men differently from women. Many laws governing work, marriage, admission to state schools, and child custody treat women and men differently.

According to Mary McHugh in *The Woman Thing*, if the Equal Rights Amendment became an official part of the United States Constitution, the following changes, and others, would occur: (1) all universities will have equal entrance requirements for men and women; (2) public schools will have to offer all classes to boys and girls — no more machine shop for boys only and home economics for girls only; (3) a married woman would be able to sell her own property and start her own business without her husband's consent; (4) child support would be based on the earnings of both parents, not just the husband; (5) laws that prevent women from working late hours (when pay is best) would be declared unconstitutional; (6) women would be eligible for the draft; (7) jail sentences would be the same for a man or a woman who has committed the same crime; (8) pregnant women could collect unemployment, if they can't find work because of pregnancy. And companies would no longer be able to refuse to hire a woman because she is pregnant.

Some women find some of these changes very frightening. For example, they believe that the protective employment laws, which say that women need not lift heavy loads or work at night, are necessary. And what about the alimony and child support and child custody laws? Phyllis Schlafly, who heads up an anti – ERA movement, says that women would lose a lot if ERA was passed. No longer would the woman "automatically" get custody of the children if there was a divorce. No longer would she "automatically" get child support payments from her husband. Under ERA, says Schlafly, a woman who could earn the same or more than her husband might have to pay him child support and alimony if there was a divorce. And then there's the question of the draft. If men and women are treated equally under the law, men and women would both be drafted. And who would stay at home with the children?

Supporters of ERA point out that "protective" laws actually work to keep women at the lower-paying jobs and that judges are already making child custody decisions according to the ability and desire of the parents to care for the children. ERA supporters also say that it isn't fair for a woman who is capable of working to sit back and collect alimony just because she was married to someone. And what about the draft? Many women have already entered the military service. And there's no reason why military service couldn't change to make room for parents with children. Perhaps men and women would work it out together if there was a draft — one of them could go and the other could stay. The government would not draft both a mother and father and leave the children alone at home.

Phyllis Schlafly is shown in a 1977 demonstration
against ERA. Her sign refers to Article 5 of the U.S.
Constitution, which has to do with how the Constitution is
amended. Ms. Carter is President Carter's wife.

OTHER ISSUES

In 1977, 14,000 women met in Houston for a National Women's Conference. Delegates to the conference tried to answer the question "What do women want?" They set twenty-five goals to work for. They outlined some of the issues important to women today, such as job training for homemakers who want it, free abortion for poor women, and Social Security benefits for housewives.

As of 1979, ERA remained one of the biggest issues of the women's movement. In some states the anti—ERA forces were very strong. After approving the Equal Rights Amendment, some states have wanted to "take back" their approval. The U.S. Supreme Court will have to determine whether states can legally take back their approval of ERA.

Abortion is another major issue. In 1972, the U.S. Supreme Court ruled that state laws banning abortion were unconstitutional. But the "Right to Life" movement, which considers abortion to be murder, was growing fast in 1979.

Laws are changing all the time, and women are continuing to work for equality. Supporters of the women's movement still have a long way to go toward achieving their goal of equality for women. But they do not seem to be discouraged by the work ahead of them.

In 1978, Bella Abzug, an active member of the women's movement, said, "The issues aren't going to go away, and neither are we. There is change everywhere. We are just beginning."

WOMEN'S LIBERATION AND YOU

Sometimes you might hear people talking about women's liberation. "Oh, I'm for equal pay for equal work," they'll say, "but I'm no women's libber!" What do they mean?

Some people believe that feminists don't like men very much, or that feminists want to *be* men instead of women. Why do they think that?

Some of the ideas of the women's liberation movement are very scary to some people. Their fathers and mothers lived a certain way; their grandparents lived the same way, too. Now some women want to turn their whole world upside down. Feminists say it's okay for women to work outside the home if they want to. They say it's okay for women to have their own friends and interests and to send their children to day-care centers. They say men should do their share of the housework. They say there's no reason why a man should be the boss of the family. But it's hard for some people to imagine changing their lives around like this. They're afraid their lives would get worse instead of better.

Feminists say that life gets better for everyone, men and women alike, when there is equality. Nobody feels pushed around. Nobody has to feel totally responsible for somebody else. People are free to be themselves.

Sometimes women become very angry at men. They think about how hard life has been for women in the past and how unfair life can be now, and they get mad. The women's movement tries to turn the energy of this anger into the energy needed to change things. Most feminists don't hate men. They simply want the same rights that men have.

Look around your school. Are boys and girls treated equally? How are they treated differently?

How do you feel about yourself? Do you feel that there are some things you shouldn't do because you are a boy or a girl? Why? What do you think would happen if you did these things? Would you be unpopular? Would you get into trouble?

Do girls play the same sports as boys at your

school? If not, why? What do boys think of girls who are good at sports? Why? Do girls ever pretend to be dumb? Why?

Not counting presidents' wives or movie stars, how many famous women do you know? How many great women are there in your history books?

What about at home? Do the boys help around the house as much as the girls? How many boys do you know who babysit?

Sometimes people get so used to doing things the same old way they forget to notice that there are other ways to do them. A lot of men and women feel that the women's movement has changed their lives for the better. Rather than living according to rigid sex roles which say that men do one thing and women do another, many people today are living freer and happier lives as individuals who are equal.

Simply having the right to *choose* one way of life or another — for both women and men — is probably the most important part of what women throughout American history have been working to achieve.

BIBLIOGRAPHY

Carlson, Dale. *Girls Are Equal Too*. Paterson, N.J.: Atheneum Publishers, 1977.

Flexner, Eleanor. *Century of Struggle: The Women's Rights Movement in the United States*. rev. ed. Cambridge, Mass.: Harvard University Press, 1975.

Friedan, Betty. *The Feminine Mystique*. New York: Dell Publishing, 1977.

Harris, Janet. *A Single Standard*. New York: McGraw-Hill, 1971.

Ingraham, Claire R. and Leonard. *An Album of Women in American History*. New York: Franklin Watts, 1972.

Lerner, Gerda. *The Woman in American History*. Menlo Park, Calif.: Addison-Wesley Publishing, 1971.

McDowell, Barbara, ed., and Umlauf, Hana, ed. *The Good Housekeeping Woman's Almanac*. New York: Newspaper Enterprise Association, 1977.

McHugh, Mary. *The Woman Thing*. New York: Praeger Publishers, 1973.

Warren, Ruth. *A Pictorial History of Women in America*. New York: Crown Publishers, 1975.